This edition 2003

Franklin Watts
96 Leonard Street
LONDON
EC2A 4XD

Franklin Watts Australia
45–51 Huntley Street
Alexandria
NSW 2015

Copyright © 1990 Franklin Watts

ISBN 0 7496 5003 6

Editor: Hazel Poole
Design: K and Co
Consultant: Michael Chinery

Printed in Italy

KEEPING MINIBEASTS

Ladybirds

Text and Photographs: Barrie Watts

CONTENTS

What are ladybirds? 6
Habitats. 8
Collecting ladybirds. 10
Handling ladybirds 12
Housing. 14
Make a net cage 16
Useful ladybirds. 18
Feeding. 20
Life-cycle 22
Completing the cycle 24
Releasing your ladybirds 26
Unusual facts 28
Index 29

FRANKLIN WATTS
LONDON•SYDNEY

What are ladybirds?

Ladybirds are colourful beetles that live in many different habitats. They can be found in gardens, mountains, meadows and deserts. Most ladybirds are red or orange with black or cream spots.

Each kind of ladybird has its own pattern with up to 24 spots. They all like to eat aphids and other small insect pests and are a great help to gardeners and farmers around the world.

Each different type of ladybird likes to eat a particular type of aphid or other insect, which means that each species of ladybird has its preferred habitat. They will mate and lay their eggs near to the aphids.

Gardens are excellent places to find ladybirds. Coniferous forests are good for certain types, but some ladybirds, like the two spot, can be found everywhere.

Collecting ladybirds

Ladybirds are only small insects so you will need only small plastic containers and a paintbrush to collect them. A warm sunny day in spring or summer is the best time to look for them.

Ladybirds move very quickly, so when you collect them, make sure that the lid of your container has airholes and is on tight. Put a leaf inside for them to cling to.

The best way to collect a ladybird is to either use a paintbrush to guide it into your box, or just let it walk onto your hand.

Never pick them up with your fingers as they can easily be damaged. When they are disturbed, ladybirds normally withdraw their legs and cling to whatever they are on. Wait until they start moving again, then you can guide them into the container.

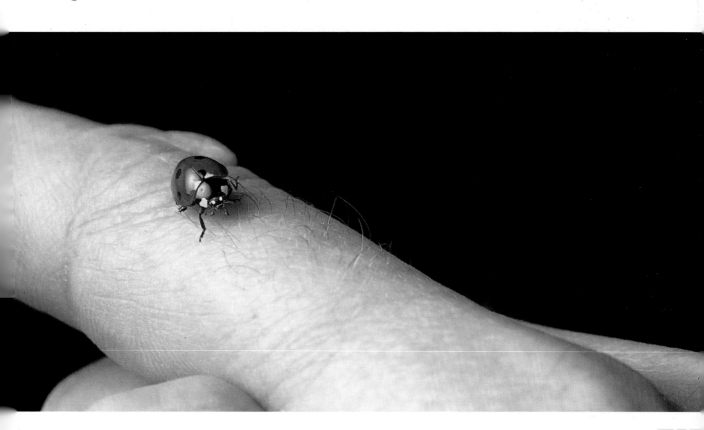

Housing

Ladybirds can easily be kept in a large clear plastic box such as an aquarium with a piece of an old sheet or similar material stretched over the top. Provide some leaves and twigs for them to crawl over and to shelter under.

Spray a little water inside regularly because
they need moisture just like other insects.
Ladybirds also need warmth so keep them on a
light and airy window sill. If not, they will hide
and you will not see them.

If you would like to breed ladybirds, the best place to do this is outside in the garden during the spring.

You can make a net cage or even buy one. Find a plant with plenty of aphids on it. Place several ladybirds on the plant and enclose it in the cage to stop them from escaping. If the cage is in a sunny position, the ladybirds will mate and lay eggs. You can study the eggs as they develop.

Useful ladybirds

When ladybirds are active, they are always looking for food. They like to feed on aphids such as greenfly which can be found on roses and blackfly which can be found on beans.

A ladybird can eat up to thirty aphids each day and the larvae (young ladybirds) can eat as many as fifty. To enable the ladybirds to breed in your cage you must give them plenty to eat.

You can collect aphids from gardens and hedgerows. Cut the stems of plants that are infested with aphids and place them in a jar of water. This will keep the plant fresh for some time so the aphids can feed on it. The aphids will breed very quickly. Each one may have several babies in a day.

Put the jar of cut food in your cage or tank. You can also brush some aphids into the cage or tank each day. Make sure that the ladybirds get a regular supply of fresh food.

Life-cycle

The ladybirds mate when the sun has warmed them and they are active. The female will lay her eggs on the underside of leaves near a supply of aphids because the tiny larvae will eat these when they hatch out.

Sometimes the larvae will eat each other if there are no aphids nearby. As they get bigger, the larvae will eat continually, searching for aphids to eat throughout the day and night.

Fully-grown larvae measure about 15mm (½ inch) long and after they have stopped feeding, they will glue themselves to the plant on which they have been hunting.

After two hours, a
ladybird larva sheds
its skin and turns into
a pupa. A few hours
later, its shell is dry
and well-camouflaged.

The adult ladybird
emerges from the
pupa after five days
and will spend the rest
of the summer
feeding. It will then go
to sleep for the winter.

Releasing your ladybirds

As ladybirds eat garden pests, it is a good idea to release them in your garden. Then you would not need to use chemical sprays to get rid of any aphids that are harming your plants — the ladybirds would control them instead.

Unusual facts

Young ladybird larvae inject saliva into their prey and suck out the contents. Older larvae are able to chew up the whole aphid.

Adult ladybirds get their spots as they dry out after emerging from the pupae.

There are about four thousand different types of ladybird living around the world.

Most ladybirds are carnivorous, that is they eat other animals. The yellow and black 22-spot ladybird is a vegetarian, and eats various plants.

Ladybirds can bite and will give a sharp nip if roughly handled.

Index

aphids 7, 8, 17, 18, 19, 20, 22

breeding 16, 19, 20

camouflage 25

eggs 8, 17, 22

food 17, 18

habitats 6, 8, 9
handling ladybirds 10, 11, 12, 13
hibernation 25
housing 14, 15

larvae 19, 22, 23, 24

mating 22

net cage 17

pupae 25

releasing ladybirds 26, 27